The Key to
Living By
Faith

KAY ARTHUR
PETE De LACY

D0062910

HARVEST HOUSE PUBLISHERS

EUGENE, OREGON

Cover by Koechel Peterson & Associates, Inc., Minneapolis, Minnesota

THE KEY TO LIVING BY FAITH
Copyright © 2009 by Precept Ministries International
Published by Harvest House Publishers
Eugene, Oregon 97402
www.harvesthousepublishers.com

Library of Congress Cataloging-in-Publication Data
    Arthur, Kay
    The key to living by faith / Kay Arthur and Pete De Lacy.
        p. cm.—(The new inductive study series)
    ISBN 978-0-7369-2306-4 (pbk.)
    ISBN 978-0-7369-3433-6 (eBook)
    1. Bible. N.T. Hebrews—Textbooks. I. De Lacy, Pete. II. Title.
    BS2775.55.A78 2009
    227'.870071—dc22

                                                                                    2008049424

Printed in the United States of America

13 14 15 16 17 18 19 20 21 / BP-SK / 14 13 12 11 10 9 8 7 6 5

CONTENTS

How to Get Started...

Reading directions is sometimes difficult and hardly ever enjoyable! Most often you just want to get started. Only if all else fails will you read the instructions. We understand, but please don't approach this study that way. These brief instructions are a vital part of getting started on the right foot! These few pages will help you immensely.

FIRST

As you study Hebrews, you will need four things in addition to this book:

1. A Bible that you are willing to mark in. The marking is essential. An ideal Bible for this purpose is *The New Inductive Study Bible (NISB)*. The *NISB* is in a single-column text format with large, easy-to-read type, which is ideal for marking. The margins of the text are wide and blank so you can take notes.

The *NISB* also has instructions for studying each book of the Bible, but it does not contain any commentary on the text, nor is it compiled from any theological stance. Its purpose is to teach you how to discern truth for yourself through the inductive method of study. Whichever Bible you use, just know you will need to mark in it, which brings us to the second item you will need...

2. A fine-point, four-color ballpoint pen or various colored fine-point pens that you can use to write in your Bible. Office supply stores should have these.

3. Colored pencils or an eight-color leaded Pentel pencil.

4. A composition book or a notebook for working on your assignments and recording your insights.

SECOND

1. As you study Hebrews, you will be given specific instructions for each day's study. These should take you between 20 and 30 minutes a day, but if you spend more time than this, you will increase your intimacy with the Word of God and the God of the Word.

If you are doing this study in a class and you find the lessons too heavy, simply do what you can. To do a little is better than to do nothing. Don't be an all-or-nothing person when it comes to Bible study.

Remember, anytime you get into the Word of God, you enter into more intensive warfare with the devil (our enemy). Why? Every piece of the Christian's armor is related to the Word of God. And our one and only offensive weapon is the sword of the Spirit, which is the Word of God. The enemy wants you to have a dull sword. Don't cooperate! You don't have to!

2. As you read each chapter, train yourself to ask the "5 W's and an H": who, what, when, where, why, and how. Asking questions like these helps you see exactly what the Word of God is saying. When you interrogate the text with the 5 W's and an H, you ask questions like these:

ᴄᴠ What is the chapter about?

ᴄᴠ Who are the main characters?

ᴄᴠ When does this event or teaching take place?

- Where does this happen?

- Why is this being done or said?

- How did it happen?

3. Locations are important in many books of the Bible, so marking references to these in a distinguishable way will be helpful to you. We simply underline every reference to a location in green (grass and trees are green!) using a four-color ballpoint pen.

4. References to time are also very important and should be marked in an easily recognizable way in your Bible. We mark them by putting a clock like this ⏰ in the margin of the Bible beside the verse where the phrase occurs. You may want to underline or color the references to time in one specific color.

5. You will be given certain key words to mark throughout this study. This is the purpose of the colored pencils and the colored pens. If you will develop the habit of marking your Bible in this way, you will find it will make a significant difference in the effectiveness of your study and in how much you remember.

A key word is an important word that the author uses repeatedly in order to convey his message to his readers. Certain key words will show up throughout Hebrews; others will be concentrated in a specific chapter. When you mark a key word, you should also mark its synonyms (words that mean the same thing in the context) and any pronouns (*I, me, my, mine; you, your, yours; he, him, his; she, her, hers; it, its; we, us, our, ours; they, them, their, theirs*) in the same way you have marked the key word. Also, mark each word the same way in all of its forms (such as *judge, judgment,* and *judging*). We will give you a few suggestions for ways to mark key words in your daily assignments.

You can use colors or symbols or a combination of colors and symbols to mark words for easy identification. However, colors are easier to distinguish than symbols. When we use symbols, we keep them very simple. For example, you could draw a red heart around the word *love* and shade the inside of the heart like this: love .

When we mark the members of the Godhead (which we do not always mark), we color each word yellow and mark the *Father* with a purple triangle like this: **Father** . We mark the *Son* this way: **Son** and the *Holy Spirit* this way: **Spirit** .

Mark key words in a way that is easy for you to remember. Devising a color-coding system for marking key words throughout your Bible will help you instantly see where a key word is used. You might want to make yourself a bookmark listing the words you mark along with their colors and/or symbols.

6. A chart called HEBREWS AT A GLANCE is included at the back of this book. As you complete your study of a chapter, record the main theme of that chapter under the appropriate chapter number. The main theme of a chapter is what the chapter deals with the most. It may be a particular subject or teaching. If you will fill out the HEBREWS AT A GLANCE chart as you progress through the study, you will have a synopsis of Hebrews when you are finished. If you have a *New Inductive Study Bible,* you will find the same chart in your Bible (page 1995). If you record your themes there, you will have them for a ready reference.

7. Always begin your study with prayer. As you do your part to handle the Word of God accurately, you must remember that the Bible is a divinely inspired book. The words you are reading are truth, given to you by God so you can know Him and His ways more intimately. These truths are divinely revealed.

> For to us God revealed them through the Spirit;
> for the Spirit searches all things, even the depths
> of God. For who among men knows the thoughts
> of a man except the spirit of the man which is in
> him? Even so the thoughts of God no one knows
> except the Spirit of God (1 Corinthians 2:10-
> 11).

Therefore ask God to reveal His truth to you as He leads and guides you into all truth. He will if you will ask.

8. Each day when you finish your lesson, meditate on what you saw. Ask your heavenly Father how you should live in light of the truths you have just studied. At times, depending on how God has spoken to you through His Word, you might even want to write LFL ("Lessons for Life") in the margin of your Bible and then, as briefly as possible, record the lesson for life that you want to remember.

THIRD

This study is set up so that you have an assignment for every day of the week—so that you are in the Word daily. If you work through your study in this way, you will find it more profitable than doing a week's study in one sitting. Pacing yourself this way allows time for thinking through what you learn on a daily basis!

The seventh day of each week differs from the other six days. The seventh day is designed to aid group discussion; however, it's also profitable if you are studying this book individually.

The seventh day is actually whatever day in the week you choose to finish your week's study. On this day, you will find a verse or two for you to memorize and STORE IN YOUR HEART. Then there is a passage to READ AND DISCUSS. This will help you focus on a major truth or major truths covered in your study that week.

To assist those using the material in a Sunday school class or a group Bible study, we have included QUESTIONS FOR DISCUSSION OR INDIVIDUAL STUDY. Even if you are not doing this study with anyone else, answering these questions would be good for you.

If you are in a group, be sure every member of the class, including the teacher, supports his or her answers and insights from the Bible text itself. Then you will be handling the Word of God accurately. As you learn to see what the text says and compare Scripture with Scripture, the Bible explains itself.

Always examine your insights by carefully observing the text to see what it *says*. Then, before you decide what the passage of Scripture *means*, make sure that you interpret it in the light of its context. Scripture will never contradict Scripture. If it ever seems to contradict the rest of the Word of God, you can be certain that something is being taken out of context. If you come to a passage that is difficult to understand, reserve your interpretations for a time when you can study the passage in greater depth.

The purpose of the THOUGHT FOR THE WEEK is to share with you what we consider to be an important element in your week of study. We have included it for your evaluation and, we hope, for your edification. This section will help you see how to walk in light of what you learned.

Books in the New Inductive Study Series are survey courses. If you want to do a more in-depth study of a particular book of the Bible, we suggest you do a Precept Upon Precept Bible study course on that book. You may obtain more information on these courses by contacting Precept Ministries International at 800-763-8280, visiting our website at www.precept.org, or filling out and mailing the response card in the back of this book.

INTRODUCTION TO THE LETTER TO THE HEBREWS

Unlike the writers of the other letters in the New Testament, the author of Hebrews does not identify himself or the letter's recipients. But the content of the letter shows us that his audience is familiar with the Old Testament, the tabernacle, the Sabbath, the priesthood, the sacrifices...his audience is Jewish. That's why this book of the Bible is called the letter to the Hebrews.

But the message of the book is not for Jews alone; it is for Christians of all backgrounds. Still, its message is built on the Old Testament, which Paul in 2 Timothy 3:15 called "the sacred writings which are able to give you the wisdom that leads to salvation through faith which is in Christ Jesus."

Hebrews will show you in a way no other New Testament book does the connection between the Old Testament and the New. It will encourage you and exhort you to live for Christ, and it will establish you in the truth of Christ's position and role in salvation.

God Has Spoken to Us in Jesus

God began speaking to Israel through the prophets more than 3000 years ago. He used many different prophets—some who spoke verbally, like Nathan, some who wrote their message, like Malachi, and some who performed miracles, like Elijah. Some combined these methods of giving God's message. They spoke "in many portions and in many ways." But "in these last days, God has spoken to us in His Son" (Hebrews 1:1-2).

DAY ONE

If you've studied any other letters in the New Inductive Study Series, you probably remember that we start by marking references to the author and recipients to see what we can learn about them, their situation, their motivations, their problems, and the like. Then we try to determine what is going on that caused the author to write the letter, and that leads us to the theme or bottom-line message of the letter.

But Hebrews is different. The author doesn't identify himself the way a classic Greek letter writer would, nor does he specifically identify his audience. Only by making note of the key ideas in the letter do you learn that the recipients were steeped in the Old Testament. And the way we note key ideas is by marking key words. So that's how we'll start. Key words repeatedly show us the key ideas and themes as well as the author's emphasis—what is most important or central to his message.

As we read and mark the text, the idea is to investigate the text. So each time you mark something key, ask the 5 W's and an H—who, what, when, where, why, and how. Read with a purpose—to discover what you can from the text. Ask questions like these: How does this sentence relate to the rest of the paragraph? Does this passage include a sequence, a comparison or contrast, or a cause and effect? To whom is the author referring?

Many of the key words and phrases occur throughout Hebrews, so list those on a three-by-five card and mark them the same way you plan to mark them in your Bible. (You can use this card as a bookmark.) Doing this as you go from chapter to chapter will help you mark consistently and save time. Remember, the point is not to fill your Bible with beautiful marks, but to unlock the author's message. Focus on what you learn, not on the way you mark. Your bookmark will not only save you time but also help you think about and process what you've read.

Read Hebrews 1 today, and mark references to *God the Father*, *Jesus*, and *angels,* as well as the word *better*. Put these on your bookmark. Many of us mark *God* with a purple triangle. The triangle reminds us of the Trinity, and purple is often a royal color, so it reminds us that God is the supreme ruler. Some people also shade the inside of the triangle with yellow because God is light. You can decide how you'll mark *God the Father*. Some use a similar symbol when marking *Son*, with the same colors and similar shape, but adding a cross. Others draw a simple cross in red to remind them of the blood Jesus shed on the cross. Choose your own symbol and/or color you want to use to mark *angels*.

Ask the 5 W's and an H as you go so you can absorb the import of what the writer is communicating.

Another way to increase your understanding of the passage is to mark time phrases. Some people mark them with a clock, and some highlight them with a color. These phrases reveal sequences and show when events occur. Mark time references in Hebrews 1. As we progress through this study, mark them in each chapter.

DAY TWO

Don't forget to begin your study time with prayer. Remember that God is the ultimate Author of the book of Hebrews and that He wants you to understand and live by every word it contains.

Make lists today of what you learn from chapter 1 about God, about the Son, and about angels. Just go through the text one key word at a time, and each time you see a marked word, write what you learn about the person or character. Keep asking the 5 W's and an H. Each item on your lists will answer one of these questions. These lists form the basis of the message about that character. Who is God? What do we learn about His character and His ways? What is the relationship between God and the Son? Between the Son and angels? The lists will show you.

DAY THREE

Did you notice how much Hebrews 1 quotes the Old Testament? In the New American Standard Bible, quotes of the Old Testament appear in the New Testament in small capital letters. One principle of Bible study is that the best commentary on Scripture is Scripture itself, so we "cross-reference." The New Testament often reveals a fuller meaning or understanding of Old Testament passages, and that's what the writer of Hebrews does here. This is called *progressive revelation*. According to 2 Timothy 3:16, all Scripture is inspired (literally, God-breathed), so we know that the New Testament revelation provides us with *God's* meaning. We don't have to make up something on our own.

Old Testament quotes help us know whom the letter was written to. If the audience were not Jews, they would not have been convinced by appeals to the Old Testament. Read these Old Testament passages:

∞ *Psalm 2*. The quotation is from verse 7, but you need to read the whole psalm to get the context.

∞ *2 Samuel 7:14*. This is part of God's covenant promise to build David's house (to establish a lineage of kings through him), but God shows us in Hebrews that it applies to Jesus.

∞ *Psalm 97:7*. The last line of the verse (in the NASB rendering) is quoted in Hebrews. The marginal note in the NASB says that it could be translated "Worship Him, all you supernatural powers."

∞ *Psalm 104:4*. Again, the marginal notes in the NASB line up with what God says through the writer of Hebrews.

∾ *Psalm 45:6-7.* This is a messianic psalm.

∾ *Psalm 102:25-27.*

∾ *Psalm 110:1.*

That's enough for today. Meditate on these things. Remember that the author of Hebrews said in verse 5 that God never said these things about angels, but He did say them about the Son.

DAYS FOUR & FIVE

Yesterday you looked at the Old Testament evidence that the writer of Hebrews presents to show the difference between angels and Jesus. Now let's look at two other New Testament passages that quote some of these same Old Testament verses and see what we learn. Read Acts 13:26-37 and Matthew 22:41-46.

How does this relate to what you recorded on day 2 about Jesus? Perhaps you're beginning to form a conclusion about one of the author's purposes or his message about Jesus.

Hebrews 1:2 tells us that Jesus is heir of all things. What does that mean? Read the parable of the landowner in Matthew 21:33-46. Who is the landowner, who is the vineyard, who is the son of the landowner, and who are the vine growers?

Hebrews 1:2,10 also tells us that God made the world through Jesus. Many people believe it was only God the Father who created the world. Some cross-references will help us find the correct interpretation. Read the following and base your conclusions on Scripture:

◦ *Genesis 1:1-2.* "God" is the English translation of the Hebrew *Elohim*, which is plural. Who moves over the waters?

◦ *Genesis 1:26-27.* What do the words "our" and "us" tell you?

◦ *Colossians 1:15-16.* This passage also explains what is meant by the "firstborn" in Hebrews 1:6.

Hebrews 1:3 tells us that when Jesus had made purification of sins, He sat down at the right hand of the Majesty on high. You'll see this twice more as you study Hebrews, but read the following and record your insights:

Matthew 19:28

Matthew 26:63-64

Acts 2:32-35

Romans 8:34

Ephesians 1:20-23

Colossians 3:1

Revelation 3:21

DAY SIX

Finally, let's look more closely at angels. People have a lot of funny beliefs about angels that aren't based on the Bible. Many of these beliefs are spread by television, movies, and popular folklore. Hundreds of Bible verses illustrate the acts that angels have done, but who are angels? What is their relationship to us? Looking at verses about a topic like this forms the basis of what is called a topical study.

Job 1:6; 2:1; 38:7 (Sons of God are angels.)

Psalm 34:7

Ezekiel 28:11-19 (This is about Satan.) *Satan*
Luke 15:10   *Balls into wickness*

1 Corinthians 6:3

2 Corinthians 11:14

Galatians 3:19

Colossians 2:18   *Matt 4:10*

1 Timothy 3:16

1 Timothy 5:21

1 Peter 1:12

1 Peter 3:22

2 Peter 2:4,10-11

Jude 6-7

Revelation 12:7-9

Now summarize what you've learned about angels.

From all you've studied this week, using a few words or a key idea from Hebrews 1, determine the theme of Hebrews 1 and record it on HEBREWS AT A GLANCE on page 107. You'll determine a theme for each chapter in Hebrews, and when your AT A GLANCE chart is done, you'll have a table of contents and handy reference tool to find certain topics or themes within Hebrews. Then at the end of our study, our AT A GLANCE chart can help us understand the main theme of the letter.

DAY SEVEN

♥ Store in your heart: Hebrews 1:3
Read and discuss: Hebrews 1

QUESTIONS FOR DISCUSSION OR INDIVIDUAL STUDY

- ∾ Discuss what you learned about angels.

- ∾ Discuss what you learned about Jesus.

- ∾ Compare Jesus to the angels.

- ∾ What did you learn about Jesus' relationship with God the Father?

- ∾ What did you learn about creation?

THOUGHT FOR THE WEEK

God says that His Son is different from the angels and different from the prophets. What makes Him different? Hebrews 1:3 says that Jesus is the radiance of God's glory and the exact representation of His nature. The Greek word translated "radiance" is used only here in the New Testament, and it means "the perfect reflection of the brightness." The Greek word translated "exact representation" means an impression on something. The idea of the two together is that God's glory, which is His nature, is impressed on Jesus exactly, so that Jesus perfectly reflects God's glory.

If we understand that Jesus perfectly reflects God's glory, we can understand better what the writer means when he says that in these last days God has spoken to us in His Son. This is important: The text does not say that God has spoken to us *through* the Son or *by* the Son, referring to what the Son has *said*. Instead, Jesus, the Son of God, is the way God speaks to us. He is the radiance of God's glory and the exact representation of God's nature. This also helps us understand John 14, where the disciple Philip asks Jesus to show them the Father. Jesus answers, "He who has seen Me has seen the Father." In other words, to ask Jesus to show them the Father was silly. They had seen Jesus, so they had seen the Father's nature.

This means that Jesus *is* what God is. That's different from saying that Jesus *has* what God has. God didn't *give* Jesus something. Instead, Jesus *is* God.

And because Jesus is God, He upholds all things by the Word of His power. He was in on creating this world and all that is in it. Genesis teaches that in the beginning, God spoke all of creation into being. God the Father, God the Son, and God the Holy Spirit created the world. John writes, "In the beginning was the Word, and the Word was with God, and the Word was God. He was in the beginning with God. All things came into being through Him, and apart from Him nothing came into being that has come into being" (John 1:1-3).

And Jesus isn't just the *Creator* of all; He is also the *Redeemer* of all. He made purification for sins. He did it Himself personally, and then Jesus, not just a prophet and not just an angel, sat down at the right hand of the Majesty on high. Prophets and angels are messengers of God's Word, but Jesus *is* the Word.

BETTER THAN THE ANGELS

Jesus is better than the angels. He has a better name and a better position. And unlike the angels, He became flesh that He might come to our aid and save us from our sins. He became like us to redeem us and rescue us from the one who held us captive under the power of death. He became our propitiation that we might live.

DAY ONE

Read Hebrews 2 and mark the key words on your bookmark. Mark *subject(ion)* and add it to your bookmark. Also mark *man*, but don't add it to your bookmark. Remember, one of the reasons we mark words is so we will slow down and read with a purpose. We're asking the 5 W's and an H so we can take in the message. The goal isn't a pretty colored page; it's a life changed by the Word of God. Marking is just a tool to help us get to our goal.

DAY TWO

Before you start making lists about what you learned, let's look a little more carefully at the chapter to be sure we've marked things accurately. Verses 5-9 could be confusing because the Bible sometimes uses the phrase *son of man* to refer to Jesus and sometimes uses it to refer to some other man (such as Ezekiel). We don't want you to be confused.

Let's start by noting the first word of verse 9. What is it? The word "but" is a marker denoting a contrast between what came before and what comes next. Contrasts and comparisons are important literary devices authors use to teach us truth. Contrasts emphasize differences, and comparisons emphasize similarities. What phrase shows up in verse 7 and again in verse 9?

Does verse 9 clearly tell us who the "Him" is?

So "Him" in verse 7 is contrasted with "Him" in verse 9, right? So who is "the son of man" in verse 7? In verses 6-8, "son of man" has one meaning, and that is contrasted with the person in verse 9. If you made a mistake in your marking, don't get discouraged. But see how important it is to read carefully?

Now it's time to list what you learned about the various characters and key words you've marked. We suggest you add to the lists you started in chapter 1 so you have a composite list of what you learned about Jesus, God the Father, and angels.

DAY THREE

Now compare what you learned in chapter 2 with what

you learned in chapter 1. Does chapter 2 reinforce the truths you saw in chapter 1, or does it reveal new things? Does chapter 2 build on chapter 1? Explain your answer.

DAY FOUR

What is the author talking about when he says that man is appointed over the works of God's hands and that all things are put in subjection under his feet? That sounds more like Jesus, but we've observed the passage carefully, and we know it's referring to man.

What world is subject to man and not angels? What about the current world?

Let's look at some cross-references about this subject, letting Scripture interpret Scripture. We need to look at the context of the whole Bible to understand the immediate context of these verses. That's an important principle: Context rules in interpretation.

Read the following passages:

> Genesis 1:26-28
>
> Genesis 3:1-8,16-19
>
> Romans 5:12; 6:23
>
> John 12:31; 16:11
>
> Ephesians 2:1-3; 6:12
>
> Ephesians 1:22-23; 2:4-7
>
> Matthew 25:31
>
> Revelation 20:4-6

Who was intended to rule the world? Who or what rules the world now, and why? What does the future hold?

DAYS FIVE & SIX

Now let's see how this idea of the world being subject to man relates to the last paragraph of chapter 2, in which the author connects Jesus to man in an important way.

How do the following passages relate to Hebrews 2:14-18?

> Romans 5:14-19
>
> Philippians 2:5-11
>
> 2 Corinthians 5:21

The word *propitiation* in Hebrews 2:17 isn't used very often today. So let's see if we can understand it from the context. From verse 17, we have the picture of the high priest offering a sacrifice for the sins of the people, and Jesus is called our high priest. But verses 9 and 14 tell us that Jesus tasted death, so He was the sacrifice as well.

Read these verses:

> John 1:29
>
> 1 Corinthians 5:7
>
> 1 Peter 1:18-19
>
> Romans 6:23
>
> Galatians 3:13

How and why did Jesus taste death for mankind? If you want a more graphic depiction of this, read Psalm 22:1-21, which portrays the true anguish of the Shepherd laying down His life for His sheep.

Think about all you've seen in Hebrews 2. Without duplicating your theme of Hebrews 1, how would you summarize

the message or theme of Hebrews 2? Record it on HEBREWS
AT A GLANCE. Use words from the text if you can, but make
it brief enough to remember, and try to capture the heart of
the chapter.

DAY SEVEN

   Store in your heart: Hebrews 2:14-15
Read and discuss: Hebrews 2

QUESTIONS FOR DISCUSSION OR INDIVIDUAL STUDY

- Discuss how Hebrews 2 relates to Hebrews 1.

- What new information do you learn about angels
  and their relationship to Jesus?

- Hebrews 2:5 says, "For He did not subject to angels
  the world to come." To whom did God subject the
  world to come? Why? When does this happen?
  How does this differ from what is happening in the
  world today? Why is the world in the condition it is?

- Discuss Jesus' partaking in flesh and blood. Use the
  5 W's and an H.

- Finally, discuss propitiation. What did Jesus do, and
  what are the implications for you? How will this
  affect your view of Jesus and your worship?

THOUGHT FOR THE WEEK

Hebrews 2 begins with an important charge to us: "We
must pay much closer attention to what we have heard, so
that we do not drift away from it." The charge is based on the

truths about Jesus in chapter 1. But the reason for the charge continues in the next few verses, asking the rhetorical question, "how will we escape if we neglect so great a salvation?" God powerfully testified to it with miracles, signs, and wonders. We didn't see these miracles, signs, and wonders personally, but the people who were alive during and shortly after Jesus' earthly ministry certainly saw them. The writer of Hebrews is saying that there is ample witness to the truth of this great salvation.

From our more distant view, many years later, do we have the same conviction? Do we believe as strongly? And do we see the greatness of the salvation we have?

A lot depends on the way we view the reality and consequences of sin. If we see that God designed man to have an intimate relationship with Him as Genesis indicates, then we must also understand the awfulness of the broken relationship we have because of sin. If we understand the just demand that sin leads to death, that the wages of sin is death, then we might begin to understand the wonder of salvation from sin.

Sometimes we lose sight of the kind of death that the Bible describes because we are all too familiar with physical death, common to all mankind now, and we are not familiar enough with eternal death in the lake of fire, which will be common to everyone who is not saved from it. Maybe we don't believe it's true.

But Jesus became flesh and blood and died for us so that we won't spend eternity in the lake of fire. That eternal state must be horrible if God sacrificed His Son to save us from it. Jesus is not only our high priest but also the sacrifice itself that propitiates the wrath of God, which exacts justice for sin.

We could not pay the price. We are not sinless. So Jesus voluntarily took on flesh and perfectly resisted all the temptations we experience so His sinless sacrifice could do the job. He became like us in birth, being born of a woman. He became like us in family, having a mother, a father, brothers, and sisters. He became like us in religious upbringing, learning the Word of God and the teachings of His Jewish faith. He became like us by experiencing the rejection of those who refused to believe the gospel. He became like us in temptation, knowing the struggle to resist blaspheming God's name by our actions and words. He became like us in suffering, enduring beatings and scourging at His trials before the Jews and Romans. He was like us in being judged by others who thought He was crazy. He was like us in being hated. And He was like us in praying for relief from agony as He did in the Garden of Gethsemane.

But unlike us, He never yielded to temptation. God made "Him who knew no sin to be sin on our behalf" (2 Corinthians 5:21). Jesus never sinned, so He was not only the perfect sacrifice but also the author (or as the King James Version says, the "captain") of our salvation. We did not initiate salvation. We did not know how to save ourselves or satisfy God's wrath. We didn't make Jesus decide to be our sacrifice, we didn't make Him take on flesh, and we didn't help Him resist temptation. All this He did on His own because of His love. His love sent Him to come to our aid. His love nailed Him to the cross. And He loved us while we were still sinners.

And by dying on the cross as that sinless sacrifice and then raising from the dead, Jesus broke the power of death. He defeated Satan, who held the power of death, and freed us from our subjection to Satan, who held us captive because of our sin. And one day, because of His resurrection, we too will reign in resurrection power in the world to come. Hallelujah!

THE HOUSE OF GOD

∿∿∿∿

"You also, as living stones, are being built up as a spiritual house" (1 Peter 2:5). You have been "built on the foundation of the apostles and prophets, Christ Jesus Himself being the chief corner stone" (Ephesians 2:20).

∿∿∿

DAY ONE

Now that you're becoming familiar with the methodology of inductive Bible study, our instructions will be briefer. Today, read and mark Hebrews 3. Mark *Moses*, *rest*, and the phrase *if we hold fast*,[1] but only add *rest* to your bookmark. You know how to mark and why we do it. (Or if you don't remember, review last week's lessons.) Keep asking those 5 W's and an H!

31

DAY TWO

List what you learn about the words you marked. Notice the contrasts or comparisons in your lists of Jesus and Moses.

DAY THREE

So far, we haven't spent much time looking at the commands given to the reader, but this chapter has quite a few. Read the chapter again and highlight or underline what we are told to do. Then go back and do the same for the first two chapters. When you're finished marking, make a list of these instructions.

Did you see any key repeated ideas in this list? What encouragement do you find? What challenges?

DAY FOUR

Another way to understand a message better is to make an outline, or at least list the key points in an argument or passage. So far in Hebrews, what or whom has Jesus been compared to? And how does Jesus compare to each? For each one, list what is true about Jesus that makes this comparison important.

Do you see a pattern of what the author is doing? Do you expect to see more of this as you go on in the book?

DAY FIVE

If you're not steeped in the Old Testament the way the original recipients of this letter were, some of these references won't make as much of an impact as the author intended. For example, the author talks about Moses being faithful, but if you don't know what might have caused Moses to give up, you can't appreciate the superior faithfulness of Jesus. Likewise, if we don't know how the people hardened their hearts and failed to enter the rest Moses promised, we might miss the challenge to not be like them.

So let's do some historical review about Moses and the children of Israel during the Exodus from Egypt and the wilderness wanderings. Read the following passages and relate what you learn to Hebrews 3:

> Exodus 3:1-8,16-17; 17:1-7
>
> Numbers 13-14
>
> Numbers 20:1-13
>
> Deuteronomy 6:23
>
> Acts 7:1-53
>
> 1 Corinthians 10:1-13

DAY SIX

What does it mean to be faithful over a "house"? Read the following verses and note your conclusions:

> Ephesians 2:11-22
>
> 1 Peter 2:4-5; 4:17

Romans 16:3-5

Colossians 4:15

And what does it mean to be a "partaker of Christ"? Read these passages and record what you learn:

John 6:48-51

John 14:16-20,23-24

Romans 8:9-11

Colossians 1:24-27

Ephesians 5:25-32

Finally today, determine a theme for Hebrews 3 and record it on HEBREWS AT A GLANCE.

DAY SEVEN

Store in your heart: Hebrews 3:14
Read and discuss: Hebrews 3

QUESTIONS FOR DISCUSSION OR INDIVIDUAL STUDY

- ∾ Discuss the comparison of Moses and Jesus.

- ∾ Discuss how Moses was faithful to his house, although the people were disobedient. You might start with simply reviewing the key points of the Exodus and then noting Moses' actions.

- ∾ What does it mean to be part of the house of God?

- ∾ What does it mean to be a partaker of Christ?

∾ Review the commands in the first three chapters of Hebrews. Which ones seem the most challenging to you?

∾ Review the contrasts and comparisons you've seen that refer to Jesus. How is Jesus superior in each case? How important are these truths? Do they change your views of anything you've read, heard, or been taught?

THOUGHT FOR THE WEEK

"If we hold fast." That phrase is used twice in Hebrews 3. The first time is in Hebrews 3:6, in which the condition "if" applies to our being part of God's house:

> But Christ was faithful as a Son over His house—whose house we are, if we hold fast our confidence and the boast of our hope firm until the end.

The second use is in Hebrews 3:14, where the condition is that we are partakers of Christ:

> For we have become partakers of Christ, if we hold fast the beginning of our assurance firm until the end.

The challenge to us is to hold fast to the end, and the condition is if we hold fast. In other words, here the writer is saying that we're part of God's house and partakers of Christ *if* we hold fast to the end. What does that mean?

It means, Beloved, that those who are of God's household, those who are partakers of Christ, *do* hold fast to the end, and those who don't hold fast to the end were never part of the house of God and never partakers of Christ. Yes, they might have been members of a church, sitting in their favorite pew or chair at worship services, participating in activities, singing songs, and quoting Scripture. But anyone can imitate these things without truly being part of God's house. Second Corinthians 11:13-15 warns us about impostors:

> For such men are false apostles, deceitful workers, disguising themselves as apostles of Christ. No wonder, for even Satan disguises himself as an angel of light. Therefore it is not surprising if his servants also disguise themselves as servants of righteousness, whose end will be according to their deeds.

Even though these deceivers are disguised, their deeds make them obvious. First John 3 tells us that the children of the devil are obvious by their lifestyles. Many today claim that you can be a child of God by believing but that your life doesn't have to change to reflect the one you belong to. These people teach that a *disciple* has a godly lifestyle and that the house of God includes believers and disciples.

But is this what John taught, or Paul, or the writer of Hebrews? Or were they saying that those who are truly partakers of Christ will show evidence in their lives? The ones who endure will reign, according to Paul's second letter to Timothy. And the same verse says the one who denies Jesus will be denied by Him (2 Timothy 2:12).

These truths are based on Jesus' own words in the Gospels. He warned us that many will say, "Lord, Lord," but He will reply that He never knew them. Continuing in the faith and not falling away in hard times or persecution—that is the evidence of your salvation. Throughout the centuries, Christian martyrs have died for their faith. Rather than recant, they were imprisoned, tortured, and killed. They endured this because they knew how great their salvation was. They knew their Shepherd, and He knew them, and no one could take them from Him. He does not lose His own. He predestined them, called them, justified them, and glorified them. From start to finish, they were His. Such is the sovereignty of God. Such is the steadfastness of true faith, true salvation, true partaking in Jesus, and being part of God's house, never to return to the kingdom of Satan.

ENTER MY REST

In six days, God completed all of creation, and on the seventh day, He rested from all His works. When God made a covenant with Israel at Mt. Sinai, He commanded them to rest from their work and keep the Sabbath on the seventh day of each week. He also commanded them to rest the land every seventh year. What does it mean to enter God's rest? Is it just a physical rest on one day out of seven? Or is it more?

DAY ONE

Read Hebrews 4 and mark the key words from your bookmark. Mark *high priest* and *faith* and add them to your bookmark. We'll be looking at the high priest for several chapters, and later in Hebrews, *faith* is used more extensively.

DAY TWO

What's our next step in study? That's right—make lists of what we learn from marking key words. That's our task for today.

DAY THREE

Another tool in interpretation is to check out the meaning of the Greek (New Testament) or Hebrew (Old Testament) words that have been translated into English. Selected word studies like this can make the text clearer. In the New Inductive Study Series, we don't ask you to do the word studies yourself, but if you're interested in learning how to find the Greek or Hebrew definitions and their meaning or grammatical implications, get *How to Study Your Bible* by Kay Arthur.*

The Greek word translated "rest" in most of chapters 3 and 4 is *katapausis*, which means "to cease from work." However, in Hebrews 4:9, the English words "Sabbath rest" are a translation of the Greek word *sabbatismos*, which is simply a Greek transliteration of the Hebrew word *shabbat* (like our English word *Sabbath*). To understand that concept better, let's do some cross-referencing and let Scripture interpret Scripture.

Read the following and note what you learn:

    ∾ Genesis 2:1-3

---

* *How to Study Your Bible* by Kay Arthur is published by Harvest House Publishers. You may obtain copies at your local Christian bookstore or by contacting Precept Ministries International at 800-763-8280 or visiting our website at www.precept.org.

∾ Exodus 20:8-11

∾ Exodus 31:12-17 (What is a sign? Who is the sign in Exodus 31 between?)

∾ Ezekiel 20:1-24 (Just read and notice how Israel responds to God.)

DAYS FOUR & FIVE

Here comes a brain stretcher, Beloved. For the next couple of days, we'll learn to reason from Scripture and use context in a way we haven't before.

The writer of Hebrews encourages us to be diligent to enter that rest so that no one will fall, so let's be sure we understand what "enter that rest" means. Let's try to answer these questions: What is that rest? How do we enter that rest?

There are three commonly held views of this rest:

1. *The faith-rest life.* This is the realization that we are simply to rest in faith and trust in the promises of God, not to strain to please Him by our own efforts, or works. Read these verses:

   Colossians 2:6-7

   2 Corinthians 5:7

   Matthew 11:28-30

2. *The millennial rest.* This is a time when Christ will rule on the earth for 1000 years and the nation of Israel will finally receive all that was promised under the New Covenant. Israel will live at rest in the promised land while Christ rules as King of kings. Read

Daniel 7:13-14,27-28 and Zechariah 14:1-9,16-21. (Not everyone believes Revelation 20 describes a literal 1000-year reign of Christ on earth.)

3. *The new heaven and new earth.* After the present heaven and earth are destroyed, peace will reign forever in a new heaven and new earth. Read these verses:

   2 Peter 3:10-13

   Isaiah 65:17-18; 66:22-23

   Revelation 14:13

   Revelation 21

So how do we determine which of these is intended— or are all three? To answer, we must stay in the context of Hebrews and ask ourselves what we've learned in chapters 3 and 4 about the rest. What would keep us from entering? And what would be the consequences of not entering? What do we do when we enter? After we answer these questions, we can determine which of these three interpretations fits the context of Hebrews best.

DAY SIX

Read Hebrews 4:12-13 and consider how these verses relate to the preceding 11 verses. Verse 12 may be familiar, but does it take on any special meaning in context?

What are the last two commands of this chapter? How does the repeated word *therefore* set up the commands? On what basis does the author declare these commands?

And what word is repeated in verse 16 that relates to

resting from works? Does this help us interpret the word *rest* in this chapter?

Record the theme of Hebrews 4 on HEBREWS AT A GLANCE.

DAY SEVEN

 Store in your heart: Hebrews 4:16
Read and discuss: Hebrews 4

QUESTIONS FOR DISCUSSION OR INDIVIDUAL STUDY

- Review the commands of this chapter. Why does the author urge his readers to do these things?

- Discuss the idea of rest and the various interpretations. Which one seems to fit the context best? Could more than one be true even though only one is intended by the author?

- What is the relationship between falling because of disobedience and the Word of God being sharper than a two-edged sword? How does God know how to judge rightly?

- Discuss what you've learned about our high priest.

- Discuss how grace relates to rest.

- Finally, what is God's lesson for us? What can we apply to our lives?

THOUGHT FOR THE WEEK

One of the most powerful images in the Old Testament

is the Sabbath. It is a hallmark of Judaism today. Even many otherwise nonobservant Jews keep the traditions of eating the Sabbath meal, lighting the Sabbath candles, and so on. Some Christians maintain that since observing the Sabbath is one of the Ten Commandments, Christians should keep the Sabbath today.

But if the Sabbath was a sign of the covenant between God and Israel (not Christians), do Christians need to observe the Sabbath as the Law demands? We are in the New Covenant, and the law is written on our hearts, not on tablets of stone. We have new hearts, hearts of flesh, replacing the hearts of stone we had. The Spirit is in us, and He leads us to obedience. The Law no longer leads us to obedience because it was only a schoolmaster, a child's tutor, to lead us to Christ. Christ has come and fulfilled the Law, so Colossians 2:16-17 gives us this instruction:

> Therefore no one is to act as your judge in
> regard to food or drink or in respect to a fes-
> tival or a new moon or a Sabbath day—things
> which are a mere shadow of what is to come;
> but the substance belongs to Christ.

We can meet for worship on any day without being judged. We can gather on Saturday as the Jews did if we wish, but we shouldn't judge someone for not doing that. The earliest records of the church (such as Acts 20:7) show that the first Christians met on the Lord's Day (Revelation 1:10), the first day of the week, or Sunday. This celebrates the resurrection of Christ.

So the particular day of the week is not the issue. What is? Is the Sabbath rest just resting on one day of seven? Or is there more? The context of Hebrews 4 says that another rest lies beyond the one that Moses and Joshua could provide.

And the rest in Hebrews 4 *remains* for the people of God, for those who have entered God's rest have also rested from their works.

The last verse of Hebrews 4 speaks of drawing near to the throne of grace so we may receive mercy and find grace to help in time of need. This must mean that our rest is more than a literal "day off" to rest from our physical toil. It must refer to a rest from working to earn salvation or God's favor. Our rest is to rest in grace. Yes, we should abound in good works. But as Titus 2:14 and 3:5-8 make clear, our works don't earn us salvation. Rather, our good works give evidence of our salvation.

James 2:14-26 tells us that faith without works is dead. Our works reveal our faith, proving that our faith is more than words.

So how did the children of Israel harden their hearts? According to Hebrews 3:18-19, they disobeyed by not believing God. So the disobedience in Hebrews 4:11 is also unbelief. We enter the rest through belief, not simply by physically resting from physical labor on a specific day of the week. Hebrews 3 and 4 describe that faith rest. Rather than trying to earn salvation by doing good deeds, we rest in faith, receiving God's grace.

Aren't you glad to know that this rest lasts for more than a day every week or a year every seven years? This rest is eternal and brings mercy and grace. This is something to rejoice about! Rejoice and be glad, and rest in the peace of knowing you're in the loving arms of a merciful and gracious Father.

A GREAT HIGH PRIEST

In the days of the tabernacle and temple, the high priest represented the people of Israel before God. Many priests offered sacrifices and interpreted the Law, but only the high priest could go into the holy of holies, and he could enter on only one day of the year, the Day of Atonement. He sprinkled blood on the mercy seat, which covered the Ark of the Covenant. But now Jesus has become our great high priest. What does this mean for us today, when there is no tabernacle, no temple, and no Ark of the Covenant?

DAY ONE

After prayer, read Hebrews 5 and mark the key words on your bookmark. Especially notice references to the *high priest*, which you've already added to your bookmark. Don't forget to ask those 5 W's and an H as you go.

DAY TWO

As our custom has been, make lists of what you learn from marking key words, again asking the 5 W's and an H.

DAY THREE

Read the chapter again and mark the phrase *according to the order of Melchizedek*. You'll see this phrase again in the next couple of chapters, so add it to your bookmark.

What three priesthoods are mentioned in chapter 5?

Make a three-column chart with these headings: Levitical Priesthood, Jesus, and Melchizedek. List what you learn about each priesthood.

DAYS FOUR & FIVE

Jacob, the son of Isaac, the son of Abraham, had 12 sons. From these sons came the 12 tribes of Israel, who inherited a portion of the promised land of Canaan. However, the descendants of one of Jacob's sons, Levi, were appointed by God to be priests for the people. Moses and Aaron were both descended from Levi, but God chose Aaron and his descendants to be the priests. All priests were Levites, but not all Levites were priests. So the priesthood is called both the Levitical priesthood and the Aaronic priesthood.

To gain a better appreciation of the forming of this priesthood, read Exodus 28–29 and Leviticus 8–9. These chapters describe the garments and consecration of Aaron and his sons.

The entire sacrificial system is laid out in Leviticus. If you want to study Leviticus, get *Teach Me Your Ways* in this New Inductive Study Series. That 37-week study briefly covers Genesis through Deuteronomy. The portion that covers Leviticus is only 7 weeks.

DAY SIX

Read 1 Peter 2:5-10 and list what you learn about the priesthood of believers. How does this compare to the other priesthoods?

Finally, determine a theme for Hebrews 5 and record it on HEBREWS AT A GLANCE.

DAY SEVEN

 Store in your heart: Hebrews 5:9
Read and discuss: Hebrews 5

QUESTIONS FOR DISCUSSION OR INDIVIDUAL STUDY

- ∞ Discuss your insights about the Aaronic priesthood.

- ∞ Compare Aaron's priesthood to Jesus' priesthood.

- ∞ Why is Hebrews 5:9 key to understanding this chapter?

- ∞ What challenge do you find in Hebrews 5:11-14? Which kind of believer are you? How do you know?

- ∞ Discuss our priesthood.

THOUGHT FOR THE WEEK

One of the most important aspects of Israel's relationship with God was the sacrificial system administered by the Aaronic priesthood. This system lasted from the Exodus to the destruction of the temple in Jerusalem by the Romans in AD 70, with a 70-year interlude between 586 BC (the destruction of Solomon's temple) and 516 BC (the building of the post-exilic temple).

Because the Jews have no temple today, they have no sacrificial system and no priesthood. They do have rabbis, or teachers, and synagogues to meet in for weekly services of Scripture readings, sermons, and prayer. However, some Jews are actively preparing new garments for priests and articles for the temple because they take very seriously the idea from the Bible that the temple will be rebuilt and the temple service restored.

This is interesting, but we Christians are not bound to that temple worship system or to that priesthood because we are not part of the covenant of the Law, which God made with Israel at Sinai. We are part of the New Covenant, which you'll see more about in Hebrews.

The priesthood of Jesus is more important to us, as we'll see in our study. We also are interested in the priesthood of believers—that's you and me! We offer up spiritual sacrifices, though they are not the physical sacrifices of the Aaronic priesthood. Like the nation of Israel, we are a chosen race, a royal priesthood, a holy nation, a people for God's own possession. And our purpose is to proclaim the excellencies of Him who has called us out of darkness into His light. We were once not a people, but now we are the people of God (1 Peter 2:9-10).

This doesn't mean that we've replaced Israel as God's chosen people, but we have been grafted into the people of

God. The New Covenant that Jeremiah 31 and Ezekiel 36 describe does not reject Israel, but according to the Gospels and Romans 11, we are included in the New Covenant.

And we haven't replaced the Levitical priesthood or the priesthood of Jesus, for He is our great high priest. But we now have a place of service as priests to God, offering spiritual sacrifices. Paul referred to this several times in his letters.

> Therefore I urge you, brethren, by the mercies of God, to present your bodies a living and holy sacrifice, acceptable to God, which is your spiritual service of worship (Romans 12:1).

> But even if I am being poured out as a drink offering upon the sacrifice and service of your faith, I rejoice and share my joy with you all (Philippians 2:17).

> But I have received everything in full and have an abundance; I am amply supplied, having received from Epaphroditus what you have sent, a fragrant aroma, an acceptable sacrifice, well-pleasing to God (Philippians 4:18).

We serve God by giving Him our lives, including our faith, our service, and our financial gifts. That's the context of Philippians 4:18. Those are the spiritual sacrifices we offer as priests. If you study the sacrifices in Leviticus, you'll see that these are not guilt offerings or sin offerings, for our guilt is removed and our sins propitiated in Christ's sacrifice. Our sacrifices are thank offerings. We offer them out of gratitude for the forgiveness and life given to us, for the mercy extended to us in Christ.

Better Hope

No one wants to live hopelessly. We all look to someone or something that will give us hope for a better tomorrow. But can we *trust* what we place our hope in? Can we have confidence? That's the hope of Hebrews 6, a hope that is an anchor for the soul, sure and steadfast.

DAY ONE

As our pattern has been now for the last five weeks, read this week's chapter (Hebrews 6), marking the key words from our bookmark. Also mark *hope* and *promise* and add them to your bookmark.

DAY TWO

Today make lists of what you learned from marking key words. Be sure to keep asking the 5 W's and an H as you go.

Also, compare the lists. What does the promise have to do with hope? How do these things relate to God?

DAY THREE

Hebrews 6 continues a thought that started in Hebrews 5:11. The chapter divisions in the Bible were added many centuries after the original writings and are man-made, not inspired by God. Sometimes we need to read the end of a chapter with the beginning of the next, ignoring the chapter break, to understand the flow of thought. So today read Hebrews 5:11–6:12.

What was the issue in Hebrews 5:11-14? How does Hebrews 6:1-2 continue that thought?

What two kinds of people are contrasted in these verses?

What two kinds of people are contrasted in Hebrews 6:4-12? Read these verses:

> 1 Corinthians 3:1-9
>
> 1 Corinthians 9:24-27
>
> Ephesians 4:11-16
>
> 1 Peter 2:1-3

How do these help you understand the contrast?

DAY FOUR

What does the author mean by "dead works" in Hebrews 6:1? Look up these cross-references:

> Isaiah 64:6

Ephesians 2:8-9

Romans 9:30-32

Galatians 3:5,10

Now, what is the value of our works (our good deeds) apart from Christ? What is "repentance from dead works"? Read these scriptures and note what you learn about repentance and salvation:

Matthew 3:1-3

Luke 13:3

Acts 2:38

Acts 20:17-21

Acts 26:15-20

DAY FIVE

Now let's turn from looking back to looking forward. Read Hebrews 6:11-20 again to refresh your memory. You marked *promise* and *hope* so you can see that these are important topics in these verses. Review your lists on these two key words.

If you're not familiar with the promise God made to Abraham, read these passages:

Genesis 12:1-2

Genesis 13:14-16

Genesis 15:4-6,18

Genesis 17:1-8,15-21

Genesis 21:1-12

Genesis 22:1-19 (this passage contains the quote in Hebrews 6:14)

That's enough work today. We'll finish this up tomorrow.

DAY SIX

The key to understanding the author's reference to Abraham's steadfastness lies in God's promise to Abraham of a seed through whom all the other promises would be fulfilled—the many descendants and the possession of the land. God promised Abraham a seed through whom all the other promises (including his many descendants and their possession of the land) would be fulfilled. Yet God asked Abraham to sacrifice his son. How could the promise be fulfilled? Abraham had to have hope. What was his hope based on? What do you see in verses 16-18?

Now, how does that relate to our promises and our hope? What is your hope based on?

How does the writer of Hebrews describe this hope? How does Jesus fit into this idea of a steadfast hope?

Record a theme for Hebrews 6 on HEBREWS AT A GLANCE.

DAY SEVEN

 Store in your heart: Hebrews 6:19

Read and discuss: Hebrews 6

QUESTIONS FOR DISCUSSION OR INDIVIDUAL STUDY

- ∾ Discuss the contrast in maturity in spiritual matters that is mentioned Hebrews 5:11–6:12. Do you see that contrast in people's lives today?

- ∾ What exhortations in Hebrews 6 speak to you? How do these help you live for Christ?

- ∾ How does Abraham's example influence your hope?

- ∾ What kind of hope does Hebrews 6 describe?

- ∾ What kind of hope do you have today? What concerns are you carrying today, and how can you apply Hebrews 6 to your life today?

THOUGHT FOR THE WEEK

Hebrews 6 included two main ideas: pressing on to maturity and having hope for the future. They are related because immature people lose hope. Mature people rest in the security of hope based on promises from God, who cannot lie.

The timeless truths of this chapter challenge us to examine our spiritual condition, our maturity, our desires, and our confidence in God. They help us make a refreshing reexamination of our relationship to God and to His Word. That's what the author intended when he wrote these words nearly 2000 years ago.

First, let's be sure we understand the message of the first half of Hebrews 6. The rest of Scripture amply indicates that our salvation is secured in God's sovereign election of us before the foundation of the world. We cannot lose our salvation. Thus, the message about falling away does not refer to losing our salvation, but to turning away from the Christlike life, turning away from the good deeds that the Gospels and letters of the New Testament abundantly encourage us to practice.

God remembers our works. He remembers our love, which John so clearly reminds us is the hallmark of a Christian, who is known by his love (John 13:35; 1 John 3:14; 4:20). James reinforces this concept with his famous "faith without works is dead" (James 2:26), reminding us that our works demonstrate our faith.

Hebrews 5–6 addresses the problem of slothfulness. Some Christians hadn't matured as they should, or the writer wouldn't have reminded them they needed milk, not solid food. He urged them to press on to maturity, to move beyond the elementary teachings that any small child would know.

And what teachings could be described as solid food? The milk is that Jesus died for your sins and rose again to newness of life and that if you believe you will have eternal life. The solid food is that this life will include suffering and that you can live through suffering victoriously. As Jesus conquered the grave, so also you are to conquer, to overcome the difficulties of life—persecution, suffering, and hardship—and maintain your faith. You maintain your faith not with words but with deeds, with a life that is based on the truth of your position in Christ, a life that is not defeated by the difficulties of life.

If your life is anchored by the hope of future eternal life with Christ, you are an imitator of Christ, who looked to the resurrection when facing the cross. This is the hope that Abraham had when God directed him to sacrifice his only son, through whom the promise was to be fulfilled. In Hebrews 11 we will see that Abraham sustained his obedience because of his hope in the resurrection power of God. His hope was an anchor for his soul.

If we do not have that kind of confidence and trust in the

promise of God, do we really confidently trust in the resurrection of Jesus? If we have trust and confidence in the resurrection of Jesus, why don't we have trust and confidence in our own lives?

If we don't have trust and confidence, we don't have hope. The biblical hope described here is not like our uncertain and wishful thinking when we hope we'll win the lottery, hope for a better job, or hope that things will turn out all right. That kind of hope is not confident because we cannot be certain about those outcomes.

Biblical hope is sure and steadfast, based on the oath or promise of God, and rooted in the character of God, who cannot lie. This is the hope of Jesus, who entered within the veil, boldly approaching the throne of grace as a forerunner for us. If we believe that Jesus did this, then we must have confidence that we have what God promised us. We might not see the fulfillment of the promise yet, as Abraham did not see it when he left Ur and then Haran. But Abraham went where God called him, confident that God would lead him to what was promised. He had biblical hope, trusting in God, who cannot lie.

That's what mature Christians are like. They live like Abraham. They have an unwavering confidence that God does not lie and that we are who He says we are, we have what He says we have, and we can do what He says we can do.

WHO IS MELCHIZEDEK?

In Hebrews 5 we learned that Jesus was "designated by God as a high priest according to the order of Melchizedek." What is the order of Melchizedek, and who is Melchizedek? We'll answer those questions in our study this week.

DAY ONE

Spend today observing Hebrews 7, marking the words on your bookmark. Make sure you mark each reference to *Melchizedek*, in addition to the phrase *according to the order of Melchizedek*.

Also mark *covenant*.[2] This key word appears frequently in the next few chapters of Hebrews. It is one of the key concepts of the Bible, so you would do well to mark *covenant* in every book of the Bible.

Now list what you learn from your markings. Pay careful attention to Melchizedek.

Today let's start on a little historical background of Melchizedek. This is cross-referencing for better understanding. Read Genesis 14 (include Genesis 13 if you have time) and make a list of all you learn about Melchizedek. Did you notice how Hebrews 7:2,5-6 helps make clear who gave a tenth to whom? The pronouns in Genesis 14:20 can be tricky—"*he* gave *him* a tenth." Scripture is the best commentary on Scripture.

In week 5 you made a chart with three columns: one for the Aaronic or Levitical priesthood, one for Melchizedek, and one for Jesus, our high priest. Today, add everything you've learned about these three priesthoods from chapter 7 on this chart. You will be collating previous lists into one chart so you can do side-by-side comparisons.

Now, who was made like whom? Was Jesus made like

Melchizedek, or was Melchizedek made like Jesus? Read Hebrews 7:3 carefully before you answer.

What characteristic of Melchizedek's priesthood matches a characteristic of Jesus' priesthood? So, what does it mean to be a priest according to the order of Melchizedek?

What are the differences between Aaron's priesthood and Melchizedek's priesthood?

DAY SIX

Now read Hebrews 7:19-28 again. Did you notice the word *better*? You first marked this in Hebrews 1 and saw it repeated in Hebrews 6. It will appear in later chapters too. So far in Hebrews, what things are better than others?

How does the discussion of hope in Hebrews 7 compare to the discussion in Hebrews 6? Is this new information or reinforcement of earlier teaching?

Hebrews 7:23-28 contains several key time indicators you should mark. What do you learn from marking time phrases in these verses? Don't miss the phrase *once for all* in verse 27. Watch for this phrase again later in Hebrews. It stands in stark contrast to *daily*[3] in this chapter.

Why is the phrase *once for all* so important when contrasting Jesus' priesthood and Aaron's priesthood?

Finally this week, record a theme for Hebrews 7 on HEBREWS AT A GLANCE.

DAY SEVEN

 Store in your heart: Hebrews 7:22

Read and discuss: Hebrews 7

QUESTIONS FOR DISCUSSION OR INDIVIDUAL STUDY

ᔆ Discuss what you learn about Melchizedek.

ᔆ Compare the priesthood of Melchizedek to that of Jesus.

ᔆ Contrast the priesthood of Jesus to that of Aaron.

ᔆ What things are described as better than others, and why?

ᔆ What difference does it make to you that Jesus holds His priesthood permanently?

ᔆ What is the significance of "once for all"?

THOUGHT FOR THE WEEK

The name Melchizedek comes from two Hebrew words: *melek* (king) and *zadek* (righteous). So his name means "king of righteousness." He was king of Salem, which means "peace." This may be a reference to Jerusalem, which was also known as Jebus, where the Jebusites lived.

Isaiah prophesied the arrival of the Prince of Peace, who we know is Jesus of Nazareth. Melchizedek is described as having no mother, father, or genealogy, so many commentators conclude that Melchizedek is a *theophany* or physical manifestation of God. Some think Melchizedek is a *Christophany* or physical manifestation of the Son of God prior to His incarnation.

But we know from Hebrews 7:3 that Melchizedek was made *like* the Son of God. The characteristic that matters in the discussion is that he holds his priesthood forever. So when God appoints Jesus to be a priest forever according to the order of Melchizedek, all the text is saying is that both of them have perpetual priesthood. This contrasts with the priesthood of Aaron, which lasts only until a man's death. This is one major point in the superiority of Jesus' priesthood over the Levitical or Aaronic priesthood.

When we get sidetracked with the notion of a theophany or a Christophany, we miss the author's point. In its place, we try to establish a point that is irrelevant to the author's purpose. However, commentators and teachers often present this idea with great conviction as if it were certain. Actually, Melchizedek is made *like* Jesus, so he can't *be* Jesus appearing in the time of Abraham. At any rate, all we need to know is that the lesser person tithes to the greater and that Jesus' perpetual priesthood is better than the temporary priesthood of Aaron and his descendants.

The key concept we don't want to miss is this: Jesus holds His priesthood forever. It's not about Melchizedek; it's about Jesus and His priesthood, which is better than Aaron's. One of the most important ideas in Hebrews for you to remember is that Jesus is *better*. He's better than the angels and better than Moses. His rest is better than Moses and Joshua's, He provides a better hope, and He has become the guarantee of a better covenant.

In fact, because Jesus is better than so many things in so many ways, we can safely say that He is better than Melchizedek too. One of the main points of the book of Hebrews is that Jesus is better than each of the things that the Jews cling to and esteem as superior to everything else in the world. Jesus is the fulfillment of all that the Old Testament offered. Paul said it best in his letter to the church at Colossae:

> Therefore no one is to act as your judge in regard to food or drink or in respect to a festival or a new moon or a Sabbath day—things

> which are a mere shadow of what is to come;
> but the substance belongs to Christ (Colossians
> 2:16-17).

Our high priest, Jesus, doesn't make sacrifices for sin daily as do the priests descended from Aaron. He made one sacrifice for sin—Himself—once and for all. That's the truth we need to hold on to in this chapter.

Jesus is better.

A New Covenant

The covenants are among the most important topics in the Bible. Studying the covenants will help you tie together the Bible as you never have before. In fact, *Testament* is just another word for *covenant*. And our Bible contains both the Old and New Testaments, or Covenants. So what is the Old Covenant, and what is the New Covenant? We'll see that this week.

DAY ONE

Read Hebrews 8, marking key words and phrases from your bookmark. As you mark *covenant* in this chapter, you'll need to distinguish between two covenants. You could mark the word *covenant* the same way each time but then add a 1 or 2 over it to show which covenant it refers to. Work carefully because this is the key idea in this chapter and the next two.

DAY TWO

Now as is our pattern, make lists of what you learn from marking key words. Add to your lists about the priesthoods. You might want to make your lists about the two covenants in parallel, as we've done before when comparing and contrasting things.

DAY THREE

Hebrews 8:8-12 quotes Jeremiah 31:31-34. So let's go to Jeremiah 31:31-34 and mark the text there. Then go to Ezekiel 36:24-28. The words *New Covenant* do not appear in Ezekiel, but the text refers to the same thing. List what you learn about the New Covenant in both Jeremiah and Ezekiel.

DAYS FOUR & FIVE

When we read Jeremiah and Ezekiel, we see that the New Covenant appears to be for the Jews—the nation of Israel. Hebrews is written to Jews who have believed in Jesus and entered into the New Covenant. But I'm not Jewish, so how does the New Covenant apply to me?

Let's look at some other New Testament passages to answer this question.

> Luke 22:1-20
>
> Acts 11:1-18
>
> Acts 13:44-48

Acts 28:23-28

Romans 1:16

Romans 11:7-13

1 Corinthians 11:23-26

Ephesians 2:13-22

Ephesians 3:4-6

Are you included in the New Covenant?

DAY SIX

You'll find an account of Israel receiving the Old Covenant, the Law, in Exodus 19–24. Read these chapters today, not pausing to mark, but just to get a better understanding or to refresh your memory.

Well, that's it for this week, Beloved! Don't forget to record the theme for Hebrews 8 on HEBREWS AT A GLANCE.

DAY SEVEN

Store in your heart: Hebrews 8:6

Read and discuss: Hebrews 8

QUESTIONS FOR DISCUSSION OR INDIVIDUAL STUDY

∞ Discuss the Old Covenant or Law.

- How did it come and to whom?

- Who is included?

- • What are the elements of this covenant?

∾ Discuss the New Covenant of grace.

- • To whom was it promised?

- • To whom did it extend, why, and how?

- • Who is included now?

- • What are the elements of this covenant?

∾ How do the two covenants relate?

THOUGHT FOR THE WEEK

When Paul wrote a letter to the church in the region of Galatia, which was located within the modern country of Turkey, he addressed the relationship between the Old and New Covenants. Many were teaching that to be a good Christian, you had to be a good Jew first, so you had to keep the Law. These teachers, called Judaizers, wanted Gentile Christians to become Jews and follow Jewish Law. They were saying that both Covenants were in effect for Christians. Some people teach that today—that if you want to be a better Christian, you should observe the Jewish feasts, keep the Sabbath, abstain from certain foods, and so on. What is the truth?

Paul labeled that teaching as a different gospel, a gospel contrary to what he had preached. Emphasizing that he was an apostle to Gentiles, he showed that the gospel he declared was not based on keeping the Law. Paul confronted those who had bought into the lie that they had to keep the Law. He called them foolish and asked them who had bewitched them. He was amazed that they had so quickly deserted Him who called them by the grace of Christ and that they had turned to a different gospel (Galatians 1:6). Paul asked them a straightforward question: "Did you receive the Spirit by the works of the Law, or by hearing with faith?" (Galatians 3:2).

How did Abraham receive righteousness? God gave Abraham a promise, Abraham believed God, and God counted it as righteousness (Genesis 15:6; Galatians 3:6). In other words, righteousness by faith came before the Law. God preached the gospel to Abraham by declaring that he would have a *seed*. God did not say the plural *seeds*, but *one* seed. And the seed God was talking about, the seed Abraham believed in, was Christ (Galatians 3:16). This was done that "in Christ Jesus the blessing of Abraham might come to the Gentiles, so that we would receive the promise of the Spirit through faith" (Galatians 3:14).

The Law, which came hundreds of years after this first promise to Abraham, did not invalidate the covenant previously ratified by God. It did not nullify the promise (Galatians 3:17). The Law was *added*. Its purpose was to define sin until Jesus came. It didn't impart righteousness, because no one could keep the whole Law. It simply declared man's sinfulness. The Law acted as a tutor or schoolmaster to teach us about sin and to lead us to Christ (Galatians 3:24-25). The goal was always for us to experience what Abraham experienced: righteousness by faith.

Righteousness has always been by faith, as God demonstrated when he declared Abraham righteous for believing God's promise. In fact, the first promise of the seed was given even before Abraham's time. Right after the fall, God promised a seed who would crush Satan's head (Genesis 3:15). That's what Jesus did. He defeated Satan, the one who had the power of death and kept men as slaves to sin. Jesus freed us from the power of Satan and the kingdom of darkness, releasing us from Satan's dominion and transferring us to His kingdom of light.

The Law was merely an addition or interlude between the covenant with Abraham and the New Covenant. The Old Covenant was fulfilled in Christ and in the New Covenant. Jesus said in the Sermon on the Mount, "Do not think that I came to abolish the Law or the Prophets; I did not come to abolish but to fulfill" (Matthew 5:17).

THE TABERNACLE

When the Israelites entered into the Old Covenant with God at Mt. Sinai, they received instructions for constructing a tabernacle—a dwelling place where God would meet with them. This tabernacle was a copy of the true tabernacle in the heavens, where God dwells, and it pointed the way to our fellowship with God now and throughout eternity.

DAY ONE

Today you'll read Hebrews 9, marking the key words from your bookmark. Mark *blood* and add it to your bookmark. Also mark references to the *tabernacle*[4] and the *holy place*[5] in the tabernacle, but don't add them to your bookmark.

DAY TWO

As usual, make lists of what you learned from your markings. This chapter will be easier to understand if you can

73

see a picture, so we've included a drawing of the tabernacle from page 1984 of the *New Inductive Study Bible*. It might be helpful if you number the parts of the tabernacle on the drawing and insert those numbers in the text of your Bible.

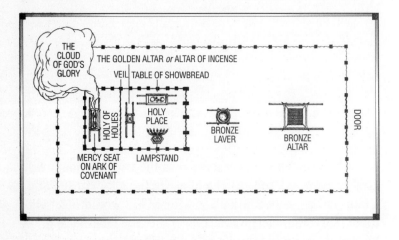

DAY THREE

The more you read Hebrews, the more you linger in its message and meditate on its precepts, the better you will understand your God and His purpose for having you study this book at this time in your life.

Today let's read the Old Testament description of the tabernacle in Exodus 25–27. This will help you understand Hebrews 9 a little better.

DAY FOUR

Cleansing was an important function in the worship system. When the tabernacle was built, it was consecrated along with all the priests. Read the descriptions in Exodus 40 and Leviticus 8.

DAYS FIVE & SIX

On the drawing we've given you, you'll see that the outer court had one entrance, which always faced east. Inside that entrance was an altar of sacrifice, on which the offerings were burned. After that was a laver full of water for washing or cleansings. Then there was a tent divided into two rooms by a veil. The first room was called the Holy Place, and the second was called the Most Holy Place or Holy of Holies. Three objects were in the Holy Place: the golden lampstand, which held seven oil lamps; the table, which held 12 loaves of bread (one for each tribe); and the altar of incense or golden altar, on which incense was burned with fire from the altar of sacrifice.

Behind the veil, in the Holy of Holies, sat the Ark of the Covenant, which held the Ten Commandments inscribed on stone tablets. Either in this box or before it were also Aaron's rod that budded and a golden jar containing some manna. Read Numbers 17:1-10 and Exodus 16:31-36 to learn about Aaron's rod and the manna.

The Ark of the Covenant was covered by the mercy seat and two cherubs whose wings pointed toward each other. (We often see the word *cherubim*, which uses the Hebrew plural ending of -*im*.) This was a portable box with rings on it to hold poles that rested on the shoulders of the Levites, who were appointed to carry it. You've already read these details in Exodus, but reviewing them is helpful.

Above the mercy seat hovered the cloud of God's glory, the Shekinah (pronounced in modern Hebrew as *shkee-nah*, with accent on the second syllable). Once a year, on the Day of Atonement, the high priest took incense from the golden altar and entered the Holy of Holies to sprinkle the blood of the sacrifice on the mercy seat to propitiate God.

These things were representative of the true dwelling place of God in heaven, and Jesus pointed to all this in His earthly ministry. Read the following verses and identify which part of the tabernacle is represented:

> Psalm 141:2
>
> Matthew 27:51
>
> John 6:33-51
>
> John 8:12
>
> John 10:9
>
> 1 Corinthians 5:7
>
> Ephesians 5:26
>
> Hebrews 4:16
>
> Hebrews 7:27
>
> Hebrews 10:20
>
> Revelation 8:3-4

These truths are so powerful that it would be good for you to memorize the layout of the tabernacle and what each piece of furniture represented. Try drawing it from memory until you have it down, and as you do, recite what each piece of furniture teaches you about Jesus or God.

Remember that the tabernacle was designed to be the means by which Israel worshipped God. Your worship of God depends on Jesus, who is the reality that these various things foreshadow—the door, the sacrifice, the cleansing water, the light, the bread, the incense, the veil, and the Ark with the mercy seat and Shekinah glory.

Reflect on what you've learned about Jesus as our high priest and our sacrifice.

Record the theme for Hebrews 9 on HEBREWS AT A GLANCE.

DAY SEVEN

 Store in your heart: Hebrews 9:22

Read and discuss: Hebrews 9

QUESTIONS FOR DISCUSSION OR INDIVIDUAL STUDY

- If you can, have a whiteboard or something to draw on big enough for the group to see, and together draw the tabernacle with all its furniture.

- Discuss cleansing (by water and by blood) and how it relates not only to the furniture of the tabernacle and to the priests but also to us.

- Discuss together what you learned about each piece of the tabernacle and how Jesus relates to it.

- Share your insights from your study of Hebrews so far about Jesus as our high priest and His role in the true tabernacle.

THOUGHT FOR THE WEEK

The earthly tabernacle was designed to lead Israel to worship God. It was patterned after the heavenly tabernacle, where God receives our worship. So what does that say about

our worship of God? We don't have an earthly tabernacle any-
more, but we do have the heavenly one. It is pictured for us in
the earthly one and made available to us by Jesus Christ.

We tend to think of worship as a service we attend at a
specific time and place. And in that service, many people
equate worship with singing. But true worship is a lifestyle. It
is the life you live according to God's Word. That's worship-
ping God in spirit and truth (John 4:23-24).

So what does that life of worship look like? The pattern is
in the tabernacle. First you must understand that you cannot
approach God except through Jesus, for He is the door.
Anyone who says there is another way to God does not worship God.

Once you acknowledge that Jesus is the only way to God,
you must understand that only His atoning sacrifice, His
shed blood, propitiates God. Without the shedding of blood
there is no forgiveness of sin. God established this pattern in
the Garden of Eden when He made coverings for the naked
Adam and Eve from the skin of animals. Blood was shed to
cover their sin. Christ our Passover Lamb was slain so that
the penalty of death would pass over us. We must live our
lives in the reality of Jesus' death on the cross for the forgiveness of our sins.

We must also know that it is the washing of the water of
the Word of God that cleanses us. We cannot approach God
without clean hands and a pure heart, and this isn't something
we can take care of ourselves. We need Christ's cleansing to
make us pure. First John 1:9 tells us that if we confess our
sins, God will forgive us and cleanse us from unrighteous-
ness. So to worship God, we need to continually confess our
sins rather than deny them.

The world of Satan is dark. Jesus, the light of the world,

dispels darkness and exposes the deeds of the wicked. Living in the light of Jesus means that we cannot participate in the deeds of darkness. As the psalmist wrote, God's Word is a lamp to our feet and a light to our path (Psalm 119:105).

The table that held the bread of the Presence reminded Israel of God's provision. Jesus Himself is the bread of life. So for us to worship God, we must feed on that bread of life. Jesus Himself taught that "man shall not live on bread alone, but on every word that proceeds out of the mouth of God" (Matthew 4:4). God's Word shows us how to live and is our sustenance, so to worship God we must be in God's Word on a daily basis.

The location of the altar of incense before the veil is a reminder that our prayers go up to God before we enter His presence. We know that whatever we ask the Father in Jesus' name, we have. So our prayers rise to the Father as a sweet aroma, and Jesus is our mediator.

The earthly high priest's path to God was blocked by the veil. But the real veil, Jesus' flesh, was torn in His crucifixion. The way to the Father is through Jesus' torn flesh and is no longer blocked. And Jesus Himself is our high priest, who enters God's presence and sprinkles the blood of a spotless sacrifice, His own blood, on the mercy seat.

And there at the throne of grace we receive mercy from God because our intercessor, Jesus, has gone before us. Our worship depends on living out these realities. Jesus is our way to the Father because of His sacrifice. His Word cleanses us, gives us light to walk by, and gives us life. We offer our prayers in His name. His atoning sacrifice tore the veil and provided the blood to sprinkle on the mercy seat so we could approach God. A life that doesn't live according to these truths is a life that doesn't worship God. Attendance at a service can be

mere window dressing and can actually make a mockery of
true worship.

Vow to live a life of true worship. Remember the tabernacle and all it represents for true worship in Jesus. Worship
God in spirit and truth.

THE BLOOD
OF THE COVENANT

What is the importance of the blood of the covenant? The writer of Hebrews has told us that "all things are cleansed with blood, and without the shedding of blood there is no forgiveness" (9:29). But we also learn that the right blood is important, because he also says that "it is impossible for the blood of bulls and goats to take away sins" (10:4). It was Christ's blood that would cleanse us, so Christ offered Himself once for all (10:10), and on that basis "we have confidence to enter the holy place" (10:19). The blood of the covenant is the blood of Jesus.

DAY ONE

Read Hebrews 10 and mark the key words from your bookmark. Also mark *sanctified*.[6] Remember to ask the 5 W's and an H. Also mark *sacrifices* and *offerings*, but mark them the same way. In some translations, you might find *believe* rather than *faith*. Mark it the same way you mark *faith*.

DAY TWO

Now make lists of what you learned from each key word you marked. Again, use the 5 W's and an H as you read. Your lists contain the answers to those questions.

DAY THREE

In Hebrews 10:5-9, the author quotes several Old Testament passages to establish that the Old Testament offerings were not what God ultimately desired. They pointed to the only sacrifice that can take away sin—the offering Jesus gave.

Read Psalm 40:6-8 and 1 Samuel 15:22 (you might need to read the whole chapter to get the context) and reflect on what God values most.

In Hebrews 10:9, what does the author mean when he says "He takes away the first in order to establish the second?" First and second what? How does this relate to chapter 9?

Compare what you learned about blood in this chapter with what you learned in Hebrews 9. Does chapter 10 reinforce old information or add new information? Why do you think the author spends so much time referring to blood sacrifices?

What sanctifies us? How are we made holy? In verse 10 the Greek word translated "have been sanctified" is in the perfect tense, which implies a completed action in the past that continues to have results in the present. By whose will have we been sanctified?

In verse 14, "has perfected" is also in the perfect tense, but "are sanctified" is a present participle. This implies that those who right now are being sanctified were perfected in the past.

What does this tell you about Christ's sacrifice nearly 2000 years ago and about our sanctification now?

How does this fit with "once for all"?

DAY FOUR

Hebrews 10:16-17 quotes Jeremiah 31:33-34. We've seen these verses in Jeremiah quoted before. What is the author of Hebrews trying to do here? Didn't he already make this point in chapter 8? Read Hebrews 10:18 before you answer.

Read verses 19 and 20. How do we have confidence to enter the holy place? What holy place? What is the new way? How is it a living way?

List the exhortations (the "let us" phrases) in verses 19-25. What are we urged to do? How do verses 24-25 depend upon verses 21-23? Compare Hebrews 10:24 to Hebrews 3:13. What are some purposes for assembling together? Do you do that in your assemblies?

DAY FIVE

Read Hebrews 10:26-31 and Hebrews 2:1-4 again. In each case, who is being judged?

Compare Hebrews 6:1-12 and Hebrews 10:32-39. What do you see?

Read Numbers 15:22-31, which shows the difference in the Old Testament between unintentional and deliberate sin. "Go on sinning" in Hebrews 10:26 is in the present tense, which implies a continuing action with duration. Read 1 John

3:6. The Greek verb tense for "sins" indicates "keeps on sin-ning."

What are your conclusions?

DAY SIX

Hebrews 10:35-39 points to the future—He who is coming will come and will not delay.

Hebrews was written after Jesus' death, burial, resurrection, and ascension to heaven, so what do these verses point to?

From what we have seen before, what does "shrink back" imply?

What do these verses teach about judgment and reward?

> Matthew 6:1-6
>
> Romans 14:10-12
>
> 1 Corinthians 3:12-15
>
> 1 Corinthians 5:9-13
>
> Colossians 3:23-25
>
> 2 John 8
>
> Revelation 22:12

Finally, Beloved, record the theme of Hebrews 10 on HEBREWS AT A GLANCE.

DAY SEVEN

 Store in your heart: Hebrews 10:10

Read and discuss: Hebrews 10

Questions for Discussion or Individual Study

∾ Discuss your insights about offerings and sacrifices in both the Old and New Covenants. What is the eternal truth?

∾ How does Jesus fit into this teaching about sacrifices and offerings?

∾ God desires obedience and not merely sacrifice. How does this affect your life?

∾ What exhortations did the author include in this chapter? How can you carry them out? Be sure to be practical and concrete.

∾ What does this chapter teach you about judgment and reward?

Thought for the Week

The Bible repeatedly refers to the future judgment of the wicked. This gives us a sense of justice when the wicked seem to get away with murder while the godly suffer for doing right. God is the judge, and vengeance is His, so we can leave that in God's hands and know that He is just.

But the Bible also talks about the judgment of the righteous. The righteous are not condemned because of their sins, for we know that our sins are forgiven and that we have been granted eternal life based on our faith in Christ. The Bible is clear that the righteous shall live by faith, so in what sense are the righteous judged?

You have studied passages concerning the judgment seat of Christ and the judgment seat of God. When the New Testament was being written, each Roman city had a raised platform in the main forum, or public space. These spaces were gathering spots for commerce and political discourse. The raised platform was known as the judgment seat. It was convenient to have this judgment seat on the edge of this public gathering place so people could assemble to hear the rulers' proclamations.

Pilate sat on the judgment seat to try Jesus. In Acts 18, Paul was dragged before the judgment seat in Corinth so Gallio, the proconsul, could hear the Jews' complaints against him. The account there and with Pilate both show that this seat was designed for ruling authorities to judge matters that were in their jurisdiction. They did not use it to judge religious matters.

So how does this apply to us? What is judged at the judgment seat of Christ or God?

The Bible is clear. This judgment determines reward or loss of reward. It is not a judgment of guilt or innocence. We are all clearly guilty of sin, but we have been declared innocent by our faith in the atoning work of Christ on the cross. His sacrifice of blood is the propitiation. He paid our debt and took on our death sentence.

But Jesus will return, and His reward will be with Him. When He does, we will stand before His judgment seat, and He will judge us according to the deeds we have done—how we lived in faith. We may receive rewards, or we may lose our reward.

What are the rewards? New Testament writers described these rewards as crowns. In 2 Timothy 4:8, Paul writes of a crown of righteousness for himself and for all who love Christ's appearing. James 1:12 and Revelation 2:10 mention the crown of life for those who persevere under trial. First Peter 5:4 tells us that elders who rule well will receive the crown of glory when the Chief Shepherd appears.

These crowns are at least part of the rewards that could

be given or lost. And why should we desire these rewards? We see the answer in Revelation 4:10, where the 24 elders fall down before the throne of our Creator and cast their crowns before His throne. This is a beautiful picture of wholehearted worship. We live our lives in faith, we persevere, and we love the Lord's appearing. We can give the crowns we receive to our Lord to show Him our allegiance and our submission. We acknowledge that all we have came from Him and belongs to Him, so we give it back to Him in worship.

Isn't that a great picture to remember? We aren't persevering in order to get; we're persevering in order to give. Our faithfulness is an act of worship that culminates in giving everything to God. That's what our everyday lives should be like—living worship of the living Word.

The Hall of Faith

The author of Hebrews has laid a theological foundation for the superiority of Christ and for salvation by faith in the gospel. Now in chapter 11, He uses the witness of saints throughout the Bible—men and women who have exercised faith—as an example to exhort all of us to press on. How will you respond to the challenge?

DAY ONE

Read Hebrews 11 today, marking key words and phrases from your bookmark.

DAY TWO

Today make lists of what you learned from marking key words. Remember to ask the 5 W's and an H with questions like these: Who were the people who had faith? How did they show their faith?

DAYS THREE - SIX

Write a synopsis of what you learned about faith. Be sure to include a definition of faith and write about the necessity of faith, the manifestation of faith, and the principles of faith that can be applied to your life.

Record the theme of Hebrews 11 on HEBREWS AT A GLANCE.

DAY SEVEN

 Store in your heart: Hebrews 11:1

Read and discuss: Hebrews 11

QUESTIONS FOR DISCUSSION OR INDIVIDUAL STUDY

- ∞ Discuss your insights about faith from your synopsis. Take your time and discuss this thoroughly. Illustrate the principles you gleaned from the examples of faith in this chapter. Feel free to refer back to any principles you learned in the preceding ten chapters.

- ∞ How will you apply these principles to your life? Be specific. Give everyone time to share at least one practical application.

THOUGHT FOR THE WEEK

> Without faith, it is impossible to please Him,
> for he who comes to God must believe that He
> is and that He is a rewarder of those who seek
> Him (Hebrews 11:6).

Do you want to please God? If you do, you need to have faith. But what kind of faith? How strong? What does faith that gains God's approval look like?

First, Hebrews 1:1-2 tells us that our faith must be based on the Word of God—what God has said. God has spoken to us through the prophets and in the rest of the Old Testament, as well as through His Son, Jesus, and the rest of the New Testament. Our faith must be based on the entire Bible, not just a few favorite verses.

Second, according to Hebrews 11:6, our faith must be assured of three things: that what God has spoken is true, that God is who He says He is, and that God rewards. How can you show that you believe God's Word is true? By remaining steadfast in the trials that test your faith. Faith that is real has been tested and proven, as we see in 1 Peter 1:6-7:

> In this you greatly rejoice, even though now
> for a little while, if necessary, you have been
> distressed by various trials, so that the proof
> of your faith, being more precious than gold
> which is perishable, even though tested by fire,
> may be found to result in praise and glory and
> honor at the revelation of Jesus Christ.

Third, faith that wins God's approval is faith that seeks Him and not the rewards or blessings of faith. Faith doesn't give us a claim on God or make Him our servant. Faith does not earn things from God, but lays hold of God and affirms, "Whatever comes to pass, You are enough."

Fourth, faith that hears and obeys God wins His approval. Faith and obedience are synonymous; unbelief and disobedience are synonymous. We've seen this here in Hebrews 11 and earlier in Hebrews 3:12,18 and 4:1-2. It's taught in James 2:19 and in Jesus' Sermon on the Mount in Matthew 7:20-21,24-27.

Fifth, faith that produces a life of righteousness wins God's approval. Righteousness is the fruit of salvation. Hebrews 10:38; 11:4,7 and 1 John 3:7,10 testify to this truth.

Last, God's approval is won with a faith that endures. In Hebrews 10:35-39, we saw that we need endurance so we don't shrink back to destruction. We have much to endure, as Hebrews 11 illustrates. We don't suffer the same trials these faith heroes endured, but some contemporary saints have been imprisoned, tortured, and even put to death. Some have had their possessions taken from them and are ill-treated. Some are constantly on the move so they can stay out of prison and continue to minister the gospel to the lost. These will gain God's approval through their faith. Will you?

RUN THE RACE
WITH ENDURANCE

The faithful witnesses of Hebrews 11 kept their eyes on the promise of the seed even though they didn't see Him. Now it's our turn to live with faith, to run the race set before us, to endure, and to keep our eyes on Jesus, following His example.

DAY ONE

Read straight through Hebrews 12 to get the flow of thought. Then go back and mark the key words and phrases from your bookmark. Also mark *discipline*, but don't add it to your bookmark. This is the only chapter in Hebrews that uses it. Remember to read with a purpose.

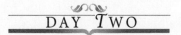

DAY TWO

Now make lists as usual, being sure to ask the 5 W's and an H so you can discover for yourself the powerful truths of this chapter.

DAY THREE

Read these passages and compare them to what Hebrews 12 teaches about discipline:

Deuteronomy 8:1-5

Psalm 119:67,71

Proverbs 3:11-12

Hebrews 5:8

James 1:2-4,12

1 Peter 1:6-9

DAY FOUR

Read Isaiah 32:17. What is the "peaceful work of righteousness" (Hebrews 12:11)?

In the context of Proverbs 4:20-27, what does Hebrews 12:12-13 mean?

Read the following verses and record what you learn about sanctification:

Matthew 5:8

1 Corinthians 6:9-11

Ephesians 5:3-7

1 Thessalonians 4:1-8

1 Peter 1:15-16

DAYS FIVE & SIX

To find out what the "root of bitterness" is, compare Hebrews 12:15-17 with Deuteronomy 29:1-21 and Acts 8:18-24.

Now let's look at Esau. Read Genesis 25:19-34; 27:1-41. What do you learn about Esau's sorrow? Read 2 Corinthians 7:9-10. What are the kinds of sorrow, and what do they produce? Compare your notes about Esau to Hebrews 6:4-8. What is your conclusion about Esau?

Finally, record the theme of Hebrews 12 on HEBREWS AT A GLANCE.

DAY SEVEN

Store in your heart: Hebrews 12:1-2

Read and discuss: Hebrews 12 (use cross-references as necessary)

QUESTIONS FOR DISCUSSION OR INDIVIDUAL STUDY

- ∾ Discuss what you learned about discipline. Pull in the cross references.

- ∾ What did you learn about sanctification and the fruit of righteousness?

- ∾ What did you learn about the root of bitterness? How did Esau's example help you understand this?

- ∾ What applications can you make in your life to all three of these major subjects? Take time to discuss these, and be compassionate and supportive as each person in your group shares.

- ∾ Discuss how you might help each other.

- ∾ Conclude in prayer about the issues each person shared and his or her desire to change.

Thought for the Week

Esau is an interesting character. The elder of twin boys, he should have held the birthright. Even today in Middle Eastern cultures, the firstborn son has preeminence in the family. To be the eldest son is an honor, but with the honor comes responsibility. He shoulders the responsibility for his mother and his siblings, even after he marries. But he also gains the wealth of the family inheritance.

If the eldest son is faithful and pleasing to his father, he also earns his father's blessing. The blessing is a public acknowledgment of approval and bestows the authority of the father on the son. The siblings understand from this that the eldest son is empowered not only by the birthright but also by the father's favor.

So what happens when the birthright is sold to a younger brother? What does that say about how the eldest son views his privileged position? Does he think he can have the blessing without the responsibility that comes with the birthright? Does he want the good things without the bad?

This idea can be challenging for us if we apply it to the issue of discipline in our lives. Do we want the blessings without the suffering, trials, and discipline? What does God tell us in Scripture? The answer is plain: The tough stuff of life prepares us, strengthens us, and builds character in us so we can handle the good stuff faithfully.

We can see this dynamic in spoiled children. When

everything is handed to children, it loses its value because the children think they deserve it, and they take it for granted. When they don't get what they want, they feel cheated, and resentment begins to build. When they don't get their way consistently, a root of bitterness begins to grow.

This kind of attitude is not godly. It isn't representative of God's children. God provides for our character first, that we might represent His character to others. So we learn gratitude for what He has given. We learn to value His gifts. We don't take things for granted or think we deserve them, because we learn to do without. We humbly depend on God instead of arrogantly making demands on Him.

Peter asks us, "What sort of people ought you to be in holy conduct and godliness, looking for and hastening the coming of the day of God?" (2 Peter 3:11-12). Jesus desires to present us, the church, as a spotless and blameless bride who hasn't played the harlot with the world. He wants us to be found worthy of His sacrifice, worthy of being adopted as children by His Father. He wants us to do good deeds because of our salvation, not because we are trying to earn our salvation or God's favor. And He wants us to receive a full reward.

The Scripture is clear that we should live in a way that pleases the Father. Our lives should reflect thankfulness and not resentment. We should not arrogantly assume that we deserve grace and mercy. Our mission is to become more and more like God in our character. We will not be the exact representation of His nature as Jesus is, but we should be as representative of God as mortal man can be while living in a human body. The writer of Hebrews declares that God has spoken to us in His Son, and we should be mindful that God expects us to speak to our world as living epistles:

> You are our letter, written in our hearts, known
> and read by all men; being manifested that you

are a letter of Christ, cared for by us, written not
with ink but with the Spirit of the living God,
not on tablets of stone but on tablets of human
hearts (2 Corinthians 3:2-3).

Press on. Run the race, laying aside every encumbrance
that can trip you up. Keep your eyes on Jesus. Follow His
example and endure discipline so you may grow more like
Him every day.

JESUS CHRIST IS THE SAME YESTERDAY AND TODAY AND FOREVER

As we bring our study of Hebrews to a close, we should remember that even though the original audience was Jewish, the truths of this book apply to a larger audience. The Jews have no tabernacle, no priesthood, and no sacrifices today, but their understanding of God hasn't changed. They know God is the same today as yesterday, and He will be the same tomorrow. So too, we must understand the unchangeableness of God and of His Son, Jesus.

DAY ONE

Read Hebrews 13, marking key words and phrases from your bookmark as usual. Also note or mark in some way each command or instruction the readers are given.

DAY TWO

Today as usual, make lists of what you learn from your marking. Consider the relationship between the commands or instructions and what you've marked. Remember, the 5 W's and an H will help you in marking, listing, and correlating what you've observed to help you understand.

DAY THREE

Hebrews 13 begins with a practical exhortation to let love of the brethren continue. Read the following passages and note what they have to say about loving the brethren. How do we demonstrate our love? How important is this to you?

Matthew 22:34-40

Luke 10:25-27

Romans 13:8-10

1 Corinthians 13:4-8

1 Thessalonians 4:9-10

1 John 3:16-19

1 John 4:20–5:3

DAY FOUR

Hospitality, even to strangers, is important according

to Hebrews 13:2. Read these verses and note how they complement Hebrews 13:1-2:

> Genesis 18:1–19:1
>
> Romans 12:9-13
>
> 1 Timothy 3:1-2
>
> Titus 1:5-9
>
> 1 Peter 4:9

How committed to hospitality are you? Do you need to change anything in your life?

DAY FIVE

Why is the command to remember prisoners and ill-treated people so important? Read the following verses:

> 1 Corinthians 12:12-27
>
> Ephesians 5:29-30
>
> Philippians 2:1-11

Our relationship to money is also important. Read these scriptures to see the full picture:

> Matthew 6:19-34
>
> Philippians 4:11-19
>
> Colossians 3:5
>
> 1 Timothy 6:6-11
>
> 1 John 2:15-17

Does your life conform to these scriptures? How can you apply them to your situation?

DAY SIX

We've come to the close of our study of Hebrews, and we could have covered so much more. This is a survey course, so we can't study each subject in as much detail as we'd like. But be encouraged, Beloved, at what you have learned. Perhaps one day you'll have time to go much deeper in this powerful book. Precept Ministries International has a more in-depth study of Hebrews in our Precept Upon Precept Series. Visit www.precept.org or call 800.763.8280 to order your copy.

Is imitating another's faith biblical? Read these verses and note what you learn:

> 1 Corinthians 4:14-17
>
> 1 Corinthians 11:1
>
> Philippians 3:17-19
>
> 1 Timothy 4:12-16

What could be the varied and strange teachings that are mentioned in Hebrews 13:9? Remember the context and read the following passages:

> Romans 14:1-4,6,14-23
>
> Colossians 2:16-23
>
> 1 Timothy 4:1-6

Do you ever hear of any varied or strange teachings today? The context contrasts them with grace. How important is grace if you want to obey God's commandments?

Finally, record the theme for Hebrews 13 on HEBREWS

AT A GLANCE. Look over your chart and determine the best way to express the central idea of the entire book of Hebrews. Record that as your book theme on HEBREWS AT A GLANCE.

DAY SEVEN

  Store in your heart: Hebrews 13:8
Read and discuss: Hebrews 13

QUESTIONS FOR DISCUSSION OR INDIVIDUAL STUDY

- Discuss all you've learned about the following:
  - your love for the brethren
  - your hospitality toward strangers
  - your care for prisoners and those who are ill-treated
  - your relationship toward money
  - your response to varied and strange teachings

- Review your HEBREWS AT A GLANCE chart and your book theme. See if you can discuss the overall flow of thought for the book—the things that Jesus is better than and why He is better.

- Leave time for your group members to share what has been the most significant truth in this book and what they would like to change in their lives.

THOUGHT FOR THE WEEK

The essence of Hebrews is wrapped up in chapter 13: Jesus is the same yesterday, today, and forever. The Jesus we know today is the same Jesus the writer of Hebrews knew and the same Jesus all those between then and now knew. And all those who follow us will know the same Jesus.

That means that Jesus has always been God. God has been speaking to us in Jesus and will continue to speak. Jesus has been, is now, and will always be better than the angels. As high priest, He has been, is now, and always will be better than any earthly priest.

The covenant we are in is better than anything that has come before because it is based on a better mediator, a better sacrifice, and better promises. This has always been true and is true now.

I can hardly imagine what life was like 100 years ago, 1000 years ago, and before that. I know what life is like today. And I know what Jesus is like today. And from Hebrews I know that the Jesus that Christians knew 100 or 1000 years ago and more is the same Jesus I know. In other words, the truths of Hebrews have sustained Christians for 2000 years.

All of us have known the same Jesus. And all of us have received the same challenge: to run the race with endurance, keeping our eyes on Jesus—that same Jesus who never changes. All of us for 2000 years have been urged to love the brethren. We all have the same charge to show hospitality to strangers. The only thing that has changed is what that hospitality looks like because homes and food and such have changed over time, just as these vary today from one place and culture to another. But the core principles have never changed.

The conditions in prisons have changed in 2000 years, but being a prisoner hasn't. How we should relate to prisoners hasn't changed. How we should relate to those who are ill-treated shouldn't change either.

We may have much more money than people had 2000 years ago, but our relationship to money hasn't changed, or at least it shouldn't have. The Word of God hasn't changed.

The things that might have changed in all these years are the varied and strange teachings. But even they are similar at their core. They give a false representation of God, of Jesus, and of salvation. They present another gospel, another way of becoming righteous in God's sight. That hasn't changed. The simple gospel often seems too simple for sophisticated people. It's too foolish for the wise, and it's too free for some—they wonder how they could receive it by faith alone. For others, it's too costly, for they aren't willing to obey God.

But Hebrews 11 challenges us with the faith of those who were willing to obey, including Abraham, who was willing to give up his promised son. Some faced impossible odds in battle. Others faced impossible odds against cruel governments who persecuted the faithful. They gave their lives because they knew that God promised a seed, and their faith in that promised seed yielded righteousness and eternal life.

Some people today who have a strong commitment to individual freedom and a strong work ethic think they have the right to believe what they want. No one will tell them what to believe, that's for sure. So they reject the doctrines of God, making themselves their own god. Others are convinced that heaven is only for those who work hard enough, do enough good works, and live a good enough life to please God. They look at the cloud of witnesses in Hebrews 11 and misapprehend the relationship between faith and works. They think that works bring righteousness, not that righteousness by faith brings works. Both groups are wrong, and both will miss heaven. Some have a false sense that they're OK with

God. Others have no security because they'll never know if their lives are "good enough."

But those who have studied Hebrews, like you, know Jesus and know their destination because of who God is, who Jesus is, and what He has done for us. We live by faith. We have our eyes fixed on Jesus, the author and perfecter of faith, and we have a cloud of witnesses from yesterday cheering us on. Run, faithful one, run with endurance.

Theme of Hebrews:

SEGMENT DIVISIONS

Author:
unknown

Date:

Purpose:

Key Words:

Jesus (Son)

God

angels

priest
(priests,
priesthood)

therefore

faith (faithful)

better
(better than)

let us

covenant

blood

hope

promise

			CHAPTER THEMES
	70ad	1	*70 ad Superiority of Christ*
		2	*Superiority of Christ*
		3	
		4	
		5	
		6	
		7	
		8	
		9	
		10	
		11	
		12	
		13	

NOTES

1. KJV: hold stedfast; NKJV: hold steadfast; NIV: hold on to, firmly;
   ESV: hold firm; also *if indeed we hold*
2. KJV: testament
3. NIV: day after day
4. ESV: tent, section
5. KJV, NKJV: sanctuary
   ESV: also *holy places*
6. NIV: made holy

$\mathcal{D}$o you want a life that thrives?

Wherever you are on your spiritual journey, there is a way to discover Truth for yourself so you can find the abundant life in Christ.

Kay Arthur and Pete De Lacy invite you to join them on the ultimate journey. Learn to live life God's way by knowing Him through His Word.

❧❦❧

Visit www.precept.org/thrives to take the next step by downloading a free study tool.

Books in the
New Inductive Study Series

✆✆✆✆

NOW AVAILABLE IN
NASB® & ESV®

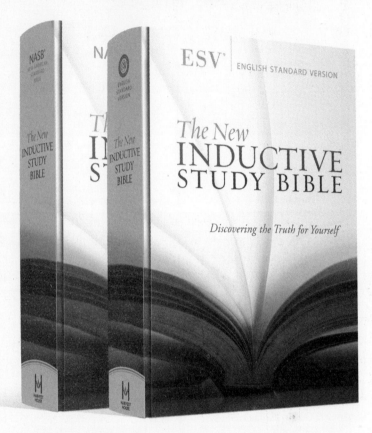

The Gold Medallion-winning *New Inductive Study Bible* (over 700,000 sold) is now available in the trusted English Standard Version. This Bible is based entirely on the inductive study approach, leading readers directly back to the source and allowing God's Word to become its own commentary.

Also available in Milano Softone™ and Genuine Leather!